FOUNDLINGS
Found Poems From Prose

DeWitt Henry

Artwork
Ruth K. Henry

First Printing — October 2023
Library of Congress Control Number: 2023938071
ISBN 978-1-953136-58-9   Hardback
ISBN 978-1-953136-57-2   Paperback

Cover Design by Kurt Lovelace
Cover Artwork by Ruth K. Henry
Cover type *Bauhaus Dessau* **Alfarn** by Céline Hurka,
Elia Preuss, Flavia Zimbardi,
Hidetaka Yamasaki, and Luca Pellegrini.
Poetry title and body set in **URW Baskerville**.
Misc. in **Jenson** by Robert Slimbach & **Sabon** by Jan Tschichold.
Flourishes set in Emigre Foundry **Dalliance**, by Frank Heine &
Emigre Foundry **ZeitGuys,** by Bob Aufuldish, Eric Donelan.
Typefaces licensed Adobe, Linotype, & URW GmbH.

PSPress.Pub
Pierian Springs Press, Inc
30 N Gould St, Ste 30
Sheridan, Wyoming 82801

To Connie
On Our 50th Anniversary

To Ruth K. Henry
For Her Art

Contents

FOUNDLINGS
Found Poems From Prose

DeWitt Henry

Artwork
Ruth K. Henry

Found poem in *"**Adventure**"*
by Sherwood Anderson

Adventure

Left by her only lover, Ned Currie,
who promised to return, but after
eleven years never did,
Alice Hindman, now 27,
came home from work
on a rainy night
to find an empty house,
her mother visiting a neighbor,
their only roomer out.

"Alice went upstairs to her room
and undressed in the darkness... .

"A mad desire to run naked
through the streets
took possession of her... .
She wanted to leap and run,
to cry out
to find some other lonely human
and embrace him... .

"Before the house
a man stumbled homeward.
Alice started to run... .
'What do I care who it is'... .

She "called softly.
' Wait!' she cried. 'Don't go away.
Whoever you are, you must wait.' "

"The man on the sidewalk stopped
  and stood listening.
  He was an old man…
  Putting his hand to his mouth,
  he shouted:
' What? What say?'…"

"Alice dropped to the ground…
  When the man had gone on his way
  she did not dare to get to her feet,
  but crawled on hands and knees
  through the grass to the house."

  Later, in her night dress, in her bed,
  she "wept broken heartedly.
' What is the matter with me?
  I will do something dreadful
  if I'm not careful,' she thought."

Found poem in *"Clytie"*
by Eudora Welty

Old Maid Gothic

The cursing was new,
and she cursed softly… .

Words which at first horrified [her]
poured in a full, light stream
from her throat,
which soon, nevertheless,
felt strangely relaxed and rested.

She cursed all alone
in the peace of the vegetable garden.

Everybody said,
in something like depreciation,
that she was only imitating
her older sister,
who used to go out
to that same garden
and curse in that same way…,
but in a remarkably
loud, commanding voice…

[Her sister now looked down
at her from her window].

When she let the curtain drop
at last, [the younger]
would be left there, speechless.

Found poem in *"**The Moons** Of **Jupiter**"*
by Alice Munro

Planetarium

A man's voice,
an eloquent professional voice
began to speak slowly
out of walls.

The dark ceiling was filling with stars.
The Milky Way appeared, was moving closer;
stars swam into brilliance and kept on going,
disappearing beyond the edges
of the sky-screen.

The voice presented the stunning facts.
A few lightyears away, it announced,
the sun appears as a bright star
and planets are not visible. A few dozen
lightyears away, the sun is not visible.

A few dozen lightyears…
only about a thousandth part
of the distance from the sun
to the center of our galaxy,
one galaxy, which contains
about two hundred billion suns.

And is, in turn, one of
millions, perhaps billions
of galaxies… .

When the show was over
I sat in my seat
while children clambered across me…

An effort had been made
to get their attention, to take it away
from canned pop and potato chips
and fix it on various knowns and unknowns
and horrible immensities,
and it seemed to have failed... .

Children have a natural immunity,
most of them, and it shouldn't be
tampered with. As for the adults
who would deplore it,
the ones who promoted this show,
weren't they immune themselves?

...they could put in the
echo-chamber effects, the music,
the church-like solemnity
simulating the awe that
they supposed they ought to feel.

Awe... once you knew what it was,
you wouldn't be courting it.

Two men came with brooms
to sweep up the debris
the audience had left behind.

Found poem in ***MRS. BRIDGE***
by Evan S. Connell

Clock

One fathomless instant
occurred on a windy, rainy night
when only she and her husband
remained at home…

For some time they had been reading,
separately;

he had the financial page
of the newspaper and she
had been idly reading of the weddings.

With the newspaper in her lap, [she]
listened to the rumbling and booming
of thunder. Suddenly, in total quiet,
the room was illuminated.

[Her husband] lifted his head,
only that and nothing more.

"Did the clock strike?" he asked.

"No, I don't believe so."

He cleared his throat.
Adjusted his glasses.
Continued reading.

She never forgot this moment
when she had almost apprehended
the very meaning of life,
and of the stars and planets,
yes, and the flight of the earth.

Found poem in *"A Loaf Of Bread"*
by James Alan McPherson

Free Lunch

Sick of complaints
about price gouging,
the corner grocer "threw up his arms
in a gesture that embraced,
or dismissed the entire store.
'All free!' he shouted... .

"A cheer went up.
The older people began grabbing,
as if the secret lusts of a lifetime
had suddenly seized command
of their arms and eyes. They grabbed

"toilet tissue,
cold cuts, pickles, sardines,
boxes of raisins, boxes of starch,
cans of soup, tins of tuna fish
and salmon, bottles of spices,
cans of boned chicken,
slippery cans of olive oil.

"Here a man, Lester Jones,
burdened himself with
several heads of lettuce,
while his wife, in another aisle,
shouted for him to drop
those small items and concentrate
on the gourmet section... .

"Others packed their arms
with detergents, hams,
chocolate covered cereal,
whole chickens with hanging asses,

wedges of bologna and salami
like squashed footballs,
chunks of cheeses, yellow and white,
shriveled onions, and green peppers.

"Mrs. Tyrone Brown
hung a curve of pepperoni
around her neck, and seemed to take
on instant dignity,
much like a person of noble birth
in possession now
of a long sought-after gem... .

"The most enterprising
fought desperately over
the three rusted shopping carts,
and the victors wheeled these
along the narrow aisles,
sweeping into them bulk items—
beer in six-packs, sacks of sugar, flour,
glass bottles of syrup, toilet cleanser,
sugar cookies, prune, apple
and tomato juices—while others
endeavored to snatch the carts... .

"There were several fistfights
and much cursing.

"The grocer, standing
behind the counter, hummed
and rang his cash register
like a madman."

Found poem in *THE THINGS THEY CARRIED*
by Tim O'Brien

Carry On

They took up what others
could no longer bear.

Often they carried each other,
the wounded or weak.

They carried infections.
They carried chess sets, basketballs,
Vietnamese-English dictionaries,
insignia of rank,

Bronze Stars and Purple Hearts,
plastic cards imprinted with
the Code of Conduct.

They carried diseases,
among them malaria and dysentery.
They carried lice and ringworm and
leeches and paddy algae and
various rots and molds.

They carried the land itself—
Vietnam,
the place, the soil—

a powdery orange-red dust
that covered their boots and
fatigues and faces.

They carried the sky.
The whole atmosphere,
they carried it,

the humidity, the monsoons,
the stink of fungus and decay,
all of it,

they carried gravity.

Found poem in *STOP-TIME*
by Frank Conroy

Library Voyeur

A girl—
I could tell by her footsteps—
[settled] in the next alcove
without seeing me.
...Chair scraped. Papers rustled.

I stood frozen...paralyzed...
that on the other side of the books
completely unaware of my proximity
a young but physically mature
female sat defenseless
in her imagined privacy... .

I moved a few books quietly
and found her, or rather
found a piece of her,
neck to breast in white cotton.

I was indeed alive,
I was who I thought I was...
nothing else mattered.

I chose to return
to the higher level of books
for another glimpse of breast...

Standing straight up
on my knees
I pressed my eye into position.

There was a moment of confusion.
I saw something. Were these fingers?
Objects I finally recognized
as hands moved away to reveal
very close, a face…

Her eyes were shut tight,
tear stained, squinting hard
as if to avoid some
overwhelming source of light.
She wept, her mouth
spread wide in a queer,
tight-lipped smile of anguish,
her head nodding slowly.

I recoiled from the peephole
as if a needle
had pierced my pupil.

Found poem in *HOMAGE TO CATALONIA*
by George Orwell

Interesting Experience

In the daytime we sniped
from no man's land…
If you waited long enough
you generally saw a khaki-clad figure
slip hurriedly across…
I had several shots…
I am a very poor shot with a rifle,
but it was rather fun.

A Facist got me instead.
The whole experience of getting hit
with a bullet is very interesting.

…the sensation of being at
the centre of an explosion.
…a loud bang…
a blinding flash of light…
a tremendous shock—
no pain, only a violent shock,
such as you get with an electric terminal;
with it…utter weakness…
being stricken and shriveled up
…sand bags receded…

All this happened [in] less than a second.
…My knees crumpled up and
I was falling, my head hitting the ground
with a violet bang which,
to my relief, didn't hurt.
I had a numb, dazed feeling.

"…Gosh, are you hit?"
"…Lift him up! Where's he hit?
Get his shirt open!" etc. etc.

…Not being in pain,
I felt a vague satisfaction.
This ought to please my wife
I thought; she had always wanted me
to be wounded, which would save me
from being killed
when the great battle came.

…When I tried to speak,
I found I had no voice,
only a faint squeak,
but at the second attempt
I managed to ask where I was hit.
In the throat, they said…
As they lifted me up
a lot of blood poured out
of my mouth, and I heard a Spaniard
…say that the bullet had gone
clean through my neck.

"The artery's gone," I thought.
I wondered how long you last
when your carotid artery is cut
…everything went blurry…
I assumed that I was killed.
And that too was interesting.

Found poem in *MADAME BOVARY*
by Gustave Flaubert

Courtship (1)

The wealthy farmer had broken his leg.
The young doctor rode from town to treat him.

The farmer's daughter
"always accompanied" the doctor
"to the foot of the steps outside the door"
while his horse was brought around.

They "stood there silent;
the breeze eddied around her
swirling the stray wisps of hair at her neck,
or sending her apron strings flying
like streamers around her waist.

"Once... she was standing there
on a day of thaw..., when tree bark
was oozing sap and the snow
was melting on the roofs.

"She went inside for her parasol,
and opened it. The parasol
was of rosy iridescent silk,
and the sun pouring through it
painted the white skin of her face
with flickering patches of light.

"Beneath it, she smiled...
and drops of water could be heard
falling one by one on the taut moire."

Found poem in *"Tell Me A Riddle"*
by Tillie Olsen

Hospice Visit

Once [her granddaughter] brought
a young Marine to visit…

gravely, without self-consciousness,
he sat himself cross-legged
on the floor and performed
for them a dance of his native Samoa.

Long after they left,
a tiny thrumming sound
could be heard where,
in her bed, she strove to repeat
the beckon, flight, surrender,
of his hands,
the fluttering foot beats,
and his low plaintive calls.

To deepen her pleasure,
he [had taken
one of the flowers sent
by friends and placed it]
in her hair. "Like a girl,"

he'd said, and brought
the hand-mirror
so she could see…

the pulsing red flower,
the yellow skull face…

she'd pushed the mirror away—
but let the flower burn.

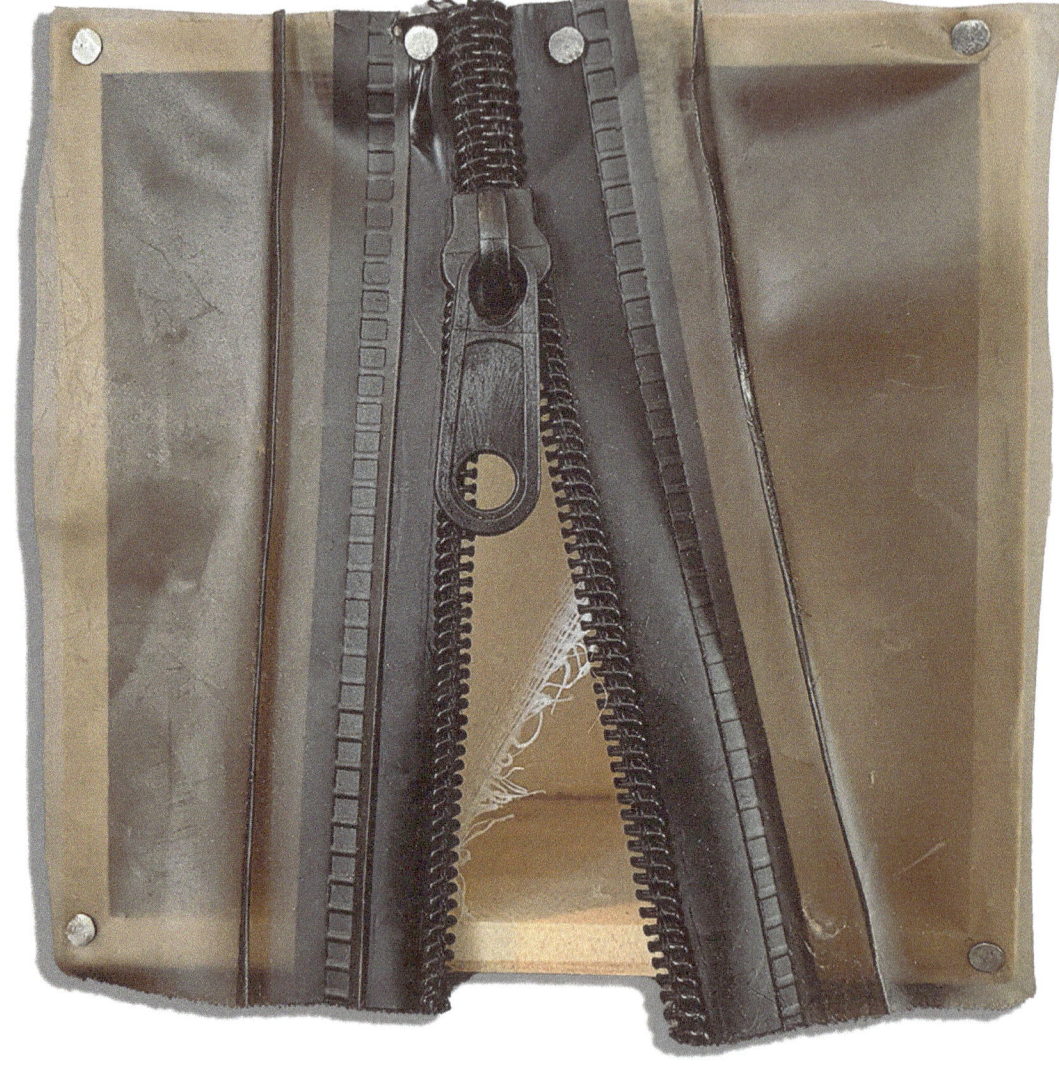

Found poem in ***"Big Two-Hearted River: Part 1"***
by Ernest Hemingway

Home Alone

"Across the open mouth of the tent
 [he] fixed cheesecloth
 to keep out mosquitoes.
 He crawled inside… light came through
 the brown canvas…

Already there was something
mysterious and homelike…
Nothing could touch him…
He was in his home
where he had made it."

War veteran, writer, and newsman,
he'd come to fish in the wilderness
of Michigan's northern peninsula,
familiar from his youth.

He'd seen the carnage and
mechanized slaughter, the worlds destroyed.
He'd been wounded. All that in Europe.

And then back "home,"
his mother had asked him to pray
and asked if he loved her.

Outside the tent, in failing light,
he built a campfire with chunks of pine,
and from his backpack, "opened
and emptied a can of pork and beans
and a can of spaghetti into the frying pan."
As it warmed on a wire grill,
and began to bubble, he mixed them together…
"There was a good smell…"
The little bubbles quickened…

He "lifted the frying pan off…
poured about half the contents out
into the tin plate… . He poured on
some tomato ketchup…
He wasn't going to spoil it all
by burning his tongue.

"Across the river in the swamp,
in the almost dark,
he saw a mist rising.
He looked at the tent once more.
… . He took a full spoonful from the plate.
'Chrise,' [he] said. 'Geezus Crise,'
he said happily."

His favorite painter was Cezanne.

Found poem in *THE MARRIAGE OF ANNA MAYE POTTS*
by DeWitt Henry

Alone In Grief

After the graveside service, they all
had left, kids busy, each with lives,
and only his bewildered now
bigger than they'd want
or he could bear to have them touch.

Day later, he picked up suit,
did shopping, cleared out medicines,
left for his daughter-in-law:
the closet, dressing table, drawers.
Clothes, donate to Salvation Army.

He needed to walk, out one neighborhood
to next, and hunched against the chill,
as if motion only searched its lack,
and world went on, and sky, and houses,
yards, and school team scrimmaging:
and live but curious and blank, and
grief alone as fact; and for moments,
nothing else, just coach and boys
and whistle blown and
one kid angling out for pass,
the world without him,
homes they'd go to, mothers cooking,
old man home form work,
all natural, enduring, and intact.

Found poem in *THE MARRIAGE OF ANNA MAYE POTTS*
by DeWitt Henry

Babysitting Nieces

Ruthie lay in an awkward sprawl;
Susan's arm dangled down.
They seemed dumped in their beds,
all in a heap, sheets kicked back,
mouths gaping, eyes sealed...

She listened to their shallow,
measured breathing, gasp and sigh,
smelled their scent.

Streetlight flickered on the wall,
on the dresser, on her then,
as she moved closer...
stood beside their bunk bed.

Susan drew her arm back, wiped her face,
turned on her back with a murmur
and jouncing the springs. Ruthie slept on.

Right knee raised, left bent out,
right arm on stomach, left
stretched out to the side,
fingers clutching sheet;
face turned towards her.

She wanted to promise them
something.... Stooped down
stealthily; reached across
and drew up Ruthie's sheet
with a slow, agonized deliberateness.

When Ruthie stirred,
she bent closer, eyes closed,
kissed her hair with a kiss
she'd never know about.

Found poem in *ANNA KARENINA*
by Leo Tolstoy

Home Birth

Levin, the young husband,
"looking at the tiny, pitiful creature,
made strenuous efforts"
to find "some traces of
fatherly feeling for it...
He felt nothing... but disgust.

"But when it was undressed
and he caught a glimpse of
wee, wee, little hands, little feet,
saffron-colored, with little toes, too;
and positively with a little big toe
different from the rest, and when
he saw [the nurse] closing the wide-open
little hands... and putting them into
linen garments,
such pity for the little creature
came upon him, and such terror
that she would hurt it,
that he held her hand back."

She laughed and told hm
not to be frightened.

Kitty asked for her baby; held
and nursed it in their bed.
She "would not let the baby go.
He fell asleep in her arms.
'Look now,' said Kitty,
turning the baby so he could see it.

55

"The aged-looking little face
   suddenly puckered up still more…
   the baby sneezed.

"Smiling, hardly able
   to restrain his tears,
   Levin kissed his wife
   and went out of the dark room."

He felt "a torture of apprehension."
A vulnerability "so painful at first…
that it prevented him from noticing
the strange thrill of senseless joy
and even pride that he had felt
when the baby sneezed."

Found poem in *WHO WILL RUN THE FROG HOSPITAL?*
by Lorrie Moore

The Good Daughter

My parents were on the front porch
when we pulled up...

two pink figures,
and I realized, showing up in front...
swollen-faced and handcuffed,

that I didn't know my parents
well enough to be doing this to them.

...It was harder to endure
the wrath and disappointment of people
who've been kept from you,
and from whom, you've kept yourself,
than it was to endure it from...
people who know you best.

All my stern upbringing was there,
waiting for me on the porch,
its unhappy administrators waiting
to administer something final and more
—or perhaps, in their failure,
to resign altogether, to take
their leave of sternness,
of administration, of me.

Found poem in ***MIDDLEMARCH***
by George Eliot

Blessed Silence

We can't "expect people
to be deeply moved by what is not
unusual. That element of tragedy
which lies in the very fact of frequency,
has not yet wrought itself
into the coarse emotion of mankind;
and perhaps our frames
could hardly bear much of it.

"If we had a keen vision and feeling
of all ordinary human life,
it would be like hearing the grass grow
and the squirrel's heartbeat,
and we should die of that roar
which lies on the other side of silence.

"As it is, the quickest of us
walk about well wadded with stupidity."

Found poem in *THE ADVENTURES OF HUCKLEBERRY FINN*
by Mark Twain

Tribute For A Poet

Emmeline Grangerford... could
rattle off poetry like nothing.
She didn't ever have to stop
to think...she would slap down
a line and if she couldn't find
anything to rhyme with it
would just scratch it out
and slap down another one,
and go ahead. She warn't
particular; she could write about
anything you choose to give her
to write about just so it was sadful.
Every time a man died, or
a woman died, or a child died,
she would be on hand with her
"tribute" before he was cold.
She called them tributes.

The neighbors said it was
the doctor first, then Emmeline,
then the undertaker—
the undertaker never got in ahead
but once; and then she hung fire
on a rhyme for the dead person's
name, which was Whistler.

She warn't ever the same
after that, but she kinder
pined away and did not live long.

Found poem *from* **"The Dead"**
by James Joyce

Insomnia

His wife had told him
about a seventeen year old boy
so obsessed with her in her youth
that he'd died of a pneumonia
caught from standing under her window
one winter night.
" 'I think he died for me,' " she'd said.

She was asleep
now, turned away in bed.

The boy had been gentle.
She'd been " 'great with him
at that time'; 'he was going to study
singing only for his health' "…
She'd written him a letter
saying she " 'was going up to Dublin
and would be back in the summer.' "
The boy had come and
stood in the garden, " 'shivering…
in the rain' "; told her
he did not want to live,
then died a week later.

"How poor a part he, her husband,
   had played in her life…

"One by one, they were all
   becoming shades. Better
   pass boldly into that other world,
   in the full glory of some passion,
   than fade and wither…

"Generous tears filled [his] eyes.

"Other forms were near...
  He was conscious of,
  but could not apprehend,
  their wayward and flickering existence.

"His own identity was fading out
  into a grey, impalpable world...

"A few light taps upon the pane
  made him turn to the window.
  It had begun to snow again.
  He watched sleepily
  the flakes, silver and dark,
  falling obliquely
  against the lamplight...

"heard the snow falling faintly...
  faintly falling."

Found poem in *"Where I Am Calling From"*
by Raymond Carver

Where He Called From

When J.P. was twelve…
he fell into a well… a dry well.
After he'd been located,
his dad hauled him out with a rope.
J.P. had wet his pants…
hollering for help, waiting,
and then hollering some more.
He hollered himself hoarse
before it was over.

…Being at the bottom of that well
had made a lasting impression.
He'd…looked up at the well mouth.
Every once in a while a white cloud
passed over. A flock of birds
flew across… it seemed to J.P.
their wingbeats set up
this odd commotion. He heard
other things… tiny rustlings
above him… which made him
wonder if things might fall down
into his hair… insects.
He heard wind blow over the well mouth,
and that sound made an impression…

everything about his life
was different for him at the bottom
of that well. But nothing fell on him
and nothing closed off that
little circle of blue.

Then his dad came along with a rope,
and it wasn't long before J.P. was back
in the world he'd always lived in.

Found poem in *WOMEN IN LOVE*
by D.H. Lawrence

Courtship (2)

She watched in hiding as
"Birkin, small and dark...
his hair tinged with moonlight,
wandered nearer." At the pond's edge,
"he stooped and picked up a stone,
which he threw sharply at the pond.

"Ursula was aware of the bright moon
leaping and swaying, all distorted...
It seemed to shoot out
arms of fire like a cuttle-fish,
like a luminous polyp,
palpitating strongly before her."

He picked up another stone.
"Then again was a burst of sound,
and a burst of brilliant light,
the moon had exploded...
and was flying asunder...

"But at the centre, the heart of all,
was still a vivid, incandescent quivering
of a white moon not quite destroyed.
It seemed to be drawing itself together
with strange, violent pangs... ."

Birkin kept stoning.
"The white fragments pulsed
up and down..., apart and brilliant...
like the petals of a rose
that a wind has blown far and wide...

"Yet again… all was still
as Birkin and Ursula watched."

He wouldn't stop. "He got
large stones, and threw them,
one after the other, …till
there was nothing but
a rocking, hollow noise,
and a pond surged up…"

He stood and listened
and was satisfied. "Ursula
was dazed… though even now,
she was aware, unseeing,
that in the darkness," the flecks
of light were "gathering a heart
again, …the cluster growing…"

They had been together; then
separated. He hadn't written.
She hadn't known that he'd come back.

She slipped from her seat
and went down to him, saying:
"You won't throw stones
at it any more, will you?"

Found poem in *"**Bungee**"*
by DeWitt Henry

Bungee

Bungee! My voice joins
the amplified, big voice
of the Bungee Master's,
as, fuck it, I surrender:

fall forward, as if to dive,
pulling the bungee coils after,
so all becomes resistless drop,
weight seeking earth, weight weightless,
plummeting, dropping, nothing
to catch, to grab, all loss and empty,
wild, let be, let, plummeting,
faster, all instants and evers,
like some years ago
slow motion of my bicycle
as the motorcycle having seen me,
pulled out anyway through a stop sign,
that awareness past avoiding,
happening, coming, coming,
then the hit as fact,
feeling rider and his cycle caving,
myself in mid-air and tumbling,
drop and impact of the street,
this is happening, bang, bang,
head on pavement,
here in middle of the road, where
cars are coming; then lying still,
waiting to discover, am I hurt,
how badly am I hurt?

Bungee like that, the plunge,
the rush and surge of ground
against elastic tug...

jerked, pulled up hard,
reverse energy heaves me
up, up, uncontrollable and dropped
to surge, and jerk, and up again,
but not as far, elastic slowed,
the up/down fading until
I'm lowered into hardness
of a safety pillow, feet
sinking into moonwalk, wading
through the rubbery, chafing,
canvas give, to the edge, where
I reach around to unbuckle
and slide off the side to solid
ground, wind blowing, normal sounds,
and nearby, idle watchers,
the un-exhilarated, inexperienced
—pygmies—as I stagger towards them.
Done. I've done it!

Found poem in *A PASSAGE TO INDIA*
by E.M. Forster

Echo Chamber

In a Marabar cave…
"Whatever is said,
   the same monotonous noise replies…
   quivers up and down the walls until
   it is absorbed into the roof.

"'Boum' is the sound…or 'bou-oum,'
   or 'ou-boum,'—utterly dull.

"Hope, politeness, the blowing of a nose,
   the squeak of a boot, all produce 'boum'"…

If one "managed to murmur,
'Pathos, pretty, courage—they exist,
   but are identical, and so is filth.
   Everything exists, nothing has value.'

"If one [spoke] vileness… ,
   or quoted lofty poetry,
   the comment would [be]… 'ou-boum.'

"If one [spoke] with the tongues
   of angels and pleaded for all
   the unhappiness and misunderstanding
   in the world, past, present, and to come…
   it would amount to the same… ."

In a Marabar cave

"…infinity and eternity
   [lose] their vastness—
   [all]…that accommodates them
   to mankind."

Mankind, (mankind), ((ou-boum)).

Found poem in *MY LIFE*
by Isadora Duncan

Alma Isadora

1

More and more my lovely body bulged under my astonished gaze. My hard little breasts grew large and soft and fell. My nimble feet grew slower, my ankles swelled, my hips were painful. Where was my lovely, youthful Naiad form? Where my ambition? My fame?

2

waiting in the night; lying on the left side the heart is smothered; turning on the right side, still no comfort; finally lying on the back; always a prey to the energy of the child; trying with one's hands pressed on the swelling body to give a message to the child.

3

Relentless, cruel, knowing no release, no pity, this terrible, unseen genie had me in his grip, and was, in continued spasms, tearing my bones and sinews apart...

4

And, on the third morning, this absurd doctor brought out an immense pair of forceps and, without an anesthetic of any sort, achieved the butchery.

5

that mouth sought my breast and bit with toothless gums, and pulled and drank the milk that gushed forth. What mother has ever told the feeling when the babe's mouth bites at her nipple, and the milk gushes from her breast? This cruel, biting mouth, like the mouth of a lover, and our lover's mouth, in turn, reminding us of the babe...Oh, women, what is the good of us learning to become lawyers, painters, or sculptors, when this miracle exists?...What did I care for Art? I felt I was a God, superior to any artist.

6

So I left Florence, giving the baby to Marie Kist to take care of...my health was in a precarious condition, and as the baby was only half-weaned, it was necessary to have the milk drained from my breasts with a little machine. This was a ghastly experience for me and caused me many tears.

7

often when I danced, the milk overflowed, running down my tunic, and causing me much embarrassment. How difficult it is for a woman to have a career!

Found poem in
"Sinners in the Hands of an Angry God"
by Jonathan Edwards

Tell It!

The God that holds you over the pit of hell,

much as one holds a spider or some loathsome insect
over the fire,
    abhors you
       and is dreadfully provoked.

His wrath towards you burns like fire.
He looks upon you
      as worth of nothing else but to be
cast into the fire.

He is of purer eyes than to bear to have you in his sight…

You have offended him infinitely
       and yet…
nothing but His hand…
      holds you from falling…

O sinner! consider the fearful danger you are in;
it is a great furnace of wrath,
       a wide and bottomless pit,
full of the fire of wrath
      that you are held over
in the hand of that God,
      whose wrath is provoked
and incensed as much against you, as against
many of the damned in hell;

you hang by a slender thread, with the flames
of divine wrath flashing about it and ready
every moment to singe it
                              and burn it asunder;

and you have no interest in any Mediation
and nothing to lay hold of
                              to save yourself,

nothing to keep off the flames of wrath,
nothing of your own,
nothing that you have ever done,
nothing that you can do

                              to induce God
to spare you one moment.

Found poem in *CLARISSA*
by Samuel Richardson

Dizgusting

"They have found another lover for me;
    an hideous one...
    None other than that Solmes!
    And they are determined, too,
    my mother with the rest!...

"[T]here was the odious Solmes
    sitting squat between my
    mother and sister, with so much
    assurance in his looks!

"...[T]he bent and broad-shouldered creature
    must needs stalk towards a chair;
    which was just by that which was set for me.

"He is a very bold, staring man!
    ...He drew it so near me, squatting
    in it with his ugly weight,
    that he pressed upon my hoop.

"...I saw what all this was for.
    I arose; the man hemming for a speech,
    rising and beginning to set his splay feet
    ...in an approaching posture.

"What are riches, what are settlements,
    to happiness? Let me not thus cruelly
    be given up to a man
    my very soul is averse to.

"...[He] snatched my trembling,
    my struggling hand; and
    ravished it to his odious mouth.

"Must I never be at liberty
    to follow my own judgment?"

Found poem in *TO THE LIGHTHOUSE*
by Virginia Woolf

Art's Dwelling

"Whatever else may perish and disappear,
  what lies here is steadfast.

"Here one might say to
  those sliding lights, those fumbling airs
  that breathe and bend over the bed itself,
  here you can neither touch nor destroy.

"What people had shed and left—
  a pair of shoes, a shooting cap,
  some faded skirts and coats in wardrobes—
  those alone kept the human shape
  and in the emptiness indicated
  how once they were filled...

"how once the looking-glass had held
  a face; had held a world hollowed out
  in which a figure turned, a hand flashed,
  a door opened... . Now day after day,
  light turned, like a flower reflected in water,
  its sharp image on the wall opposite.

"Only the shadows of the trees,
  flourishing in the wind,
  made obeisance on the wall,
  and for a moment darkened the pool
  in which light reflected itself;
  or birds, flying, made a soft spot
  flutter slowly across the bedroom floor..."

The care-taker arrived. Tore "the veil
of silence with hands that had stood
in the wash-tub, grinding with boots
that had crunched the shingle,
came as directed to open
all windows, and dust the bedroom.

"How long, she asked, creaking and
groaning on her knees under the bed,
dusting the boards, how shall it endure?
It was beyond the strength of one woman,
she said. They never sent… never wrote…
The place was gone to rack and ruin."

For ten years after the mother's death,
the father, eight children, and their friends had
gone their ways, through war and lives.
One daughter married. "[D]reams persisted…
[T]hat good triumphs, happiness prevails,
order rules." But then she'd died in childbirth,
followed by the oldest brother, "blown up in France."

A surprise note from "one of the young ladies,"
told the care-taker to ready the house.
"They might be coming for the summer":
the father, children, and friends "expected
to find things as they had left them."

A second house keeper and her son helped.
All in a hurry. They "stayed the corruption
and the rot"; scythed the yard.
Builders made repairs. A cook came.

The old gentleman, family, and guests arrived.
An older writer. A woman painter. Others.
They'd had up to twenty guests before.
And now again, "The house was full."
As for the world, Peace had returned.
Family, nation, and spirit were revived.

The mother's mission to deliver gifts
to a distant lighthouse for its keeper
and his sickly son—prevented ten years
before by bad weather—was now completed
by the father and surviving children; as was
the canvas portraying them by the artist.

" 'You' and 'I' and 'she' pass and vanish,"
but not art; "or at least not what it attempts,"
the painter mused, leaving us to our visions.

Found poem in
"Letter to Lord Chesterfield, February 7, 1755"
by Samuel Johnson

Support The Arts

Is not a patron,
my lord,
one who looks
with unconcern
on a man

struggling for life
in the water,

and when
he has reached ground

encumbers him
with help?

*

The notice you have taken
of my labors

had it been early
had been kind;

but it has been delayed

till I am indifferent,
and cannot enjoy it;

till I am solitary,
and cannot impart it;

till I am known,
and do not want it.

Found poems in *DEATH OF THE HEART*
by Elizabeth Bowen

Out Of Sight

The senses bound our feeling world:
there is an abrupt break
where their power stops—

when the door closes, the train disappears
round the curve, the plane's droning
becomes inaudible, the ship
enters the mists or drops
over the line of the sea.

The heart may think it knows better;
the senses know that absence blots
people out. We have really no absent friends.

The friend becomes a traitor
by breaking, however unwillingly or sadly,
out of our own zone: a hard judgment
is passed on him, for all the pleas of the heart.

Willing absence (however unwilling)
is the negation of love. To remember
can be at times no more than a cold duty,
for we remember only in the limited way
that is bearable. We observe small rites,
but we defend ourselves against
that terrible memory that is stronger than will.

We defend ourselves from the rooms,
the scenes, the objects that make for hallucinations,
that make the senses start up and fasten upon a ghost.

We desert those who desert us;
we cannot afford to suffer;
we must live how we can.

Found poems in *DEATH OF THE HEART*
by Elizabeth Bowen

Sorrow's Company

The aristocratic privilege of silence
belongs, you soon find out,
to only the happy state—or, at least, to the state
when pain keeps within bounds.

With its accession to full power,
feeling becomes subversive and violent:
the proud part of the nature is battered down.

Then those people who flock to the scenes
of accidents, who love most of all to dwell
on deaths or childbirths or on the sick-bed
from which restraint has gone…
are on the spot at once, pressing close…

They bring with them the sense that
the most individual sorrow
has a a stupefying universality.

In them, human nature makes felt
its clumsy wisdom, it efficacy,
its infallible ready reckoning, its lower level
from which there is no further to drop…

The proper comment on grief,
that comment that returns it to poetry,
comes not in the right words,
the faultless, perceptive silence,

but from the chorus of vulgar,
unsought friends—friends who are strangers
to the taste and the mind.

Found poem in *GULLIVER'S TRAVELS*
by Jonathan Swift

From The Horse's Mouth

> "I had rather have a fool to make me merry
>   than experience to make me sad—and to
>   travel for it, too."
>
>   Rosalind, *"As You Like It"*

After trying to describe
our Euro-concept of war to my master,
a sage in peaceful Houyhnhnm land,

how wars began with the greed of princes,
or with differences of opinions—

or how "sometimes our neighbors want
the things we have, or have the things
we want; and we both fight…"

How we've invented weapons, including
"cannons, culverins, muskets, carabines,
pistols, bullets, powder, swords, bayonets";

how we make "battles, sieges, retreats, attacks,"
use "undermines, countermines, bombardments,"
have "sea-fights; ships sunk with a thousand men,
twenty thousand killed on each side";

how we suffer "dying groans, limbs flying in the air,
smoke, noise, confusion, trampling to death
under horses' feet; flight, pursuit, victory;
fields strewed with carcases left for food
to dogs, and wolves, and birds of prey…"

—my master remarked:

"That although he hated the yahoos
   of [his own country], yet he no more
   blamed them for their odious qualities,
   than he did a gnnah (a bird of prey) for its cruelty,
   or a sharp stone for cutting his hoof.

"But when a creature pretending to reason"—
   such as me and my European breed—
"could be capable of such enormities,
   he dreaded lest the corruption of that faculty
   might be worse than brutality itself.

"He seemed therefore confident,
   that instead of reason,
   we were only possessed of some quality
   fitted to increase our natural vices,

"as the reflection from a troubled stream
   returns the image of an ill-shaped
   body; not only larger, but more distorted."

   I had hoped to stay with Houyhnhnms
   forever, but was banished after three years
   by reason of flawed nature.

Their council had decided,
and even my master finally agreed.
A yahoo was a yahoo, however "wonderful."

He said, "yahoos were known to hate
one another more than they did
any different species of animals;
and the reason usually assigned
was the odiousness of their own shapes,
which all could see in the rest,
but not in themselves."

I had to build a canoe and set sail
again into the ocean's vast indifference.

I did reach home, but found
even my family disgusted me.
I'd learned self-hate.

Proudly, I exempted myself from pride,
the greatest fault of yahoos,
and bought two horses for companions.

Except: except for love,
why write my travels?
Houyhnhnms have no need to read.
It's you dear reader that I seek.

Found poem in *"You Must Remember This"*
by Robert Coover

Casablanca's Missing Sex Scene

"I luff you, Richard!"
  [Ilsa] declares breathlessly,
  though she seems to be speaking...
  not to him, but to the ceiling,
  if there is one up there.

"His eyes too are closed now.
  his hands gripping her soft hips,
  pulling her down...

"Rick Blaine, a man annealed
  to loneliness and betrayal,
  but flawed—hopelessly, it seems—
  by hope itself.

"He is, in the tragic sense,
  a true revolutionary:
  his gaping mouth bespeaks this,
  the spittle in the corners
  of his lips, his eyes, open now
  and staring into some
  infinite distance not unlike
  the future, his knitted brow.

"He heaves upward, impaling her
  to the very core: 'Oh. Gott!' she screams,
  her back arching, mouth agape
  as though to commence
'La Marseillaisle.'

"...This is love
   in all its clammy mystery,
   the ultimate connection..."

[Whatever else it seems, or doesn't,
Ilsa wins the letters of transit
for herself and her husband,
the French Resistance leader;

while Rick, having performed
a Kama Sutra of porn cliches,
begins a beautiful friendship
with the head Vichy cop.]

Found poem in *MY BROTHER*
by Jamaica Kincaid

Such A Thing

[Death] happens every day,
but when you see the mourners,
they behave as if it were so new,
this event, death, dying—
someone you love dies—
it has never happened before...

*

...after [my brother] was buried
in the warm and yellow clay
of Antigua, I resumed the life
that his death had interrupted,

the life with my own family,
and the life of having written a book
and persuading people
to simply go and buy it.

[I traveled to Chicago for a reading
and never told people]
that I was in a state of pain...
I did not know how to explain;

such a thing had never
happened to me before

*

In spite of all the people
I had been close to who had died
I had never believed in it,
the very fact that they had died;
...I thought of them as somewhere else.

[But I had viewed my brother
in a plastic bag, unzipped.]
He did not look like my brother…
His hairs uncombed, face unshaven,
his eyes were open wide,
and his mouth was wide-open, too…

as if he were screaming…
and this scream seemed to have
no break in it;
this scream only came out
in one exhalation,
trailing off into eternity,
or just trailing off somewhere
I do not know,
or just trailing off into nothing.

Someone I did not know I loved
had died, and that dying
had a closed-door quality to it,
a falling-off-the-horizon quality to it,
the end, an end, nothing…

and yet, what to do?

Found poem in *THE WESTERN CANON*
by Harold Bloom,
who found it in *"The Theme of the Three Caskets"*
by Sigmund Freud
who found it in Shakespeare's *KING LEAR*

Shakespeare Writes
Freud Writes
Harold Bloom

"Eternal wisdom
  ...bids the old man
  renounce love,
  choose death,
  and make friends
  with the necessity
  of dying...

"[Man has] three
  inevitable relations
  with women:

"the mother who bears him,
  the companion of
  his bed and board,
  and with the destroyer...

"[I]t is vain
  that the old man yearns
  after the love of woman
  as he had it from his mother;
  the third of the Fates alone,
  the silent goddess of Death,
  will take him into her arms."

Finder's Note

Quotes from writers copyrighted since 1926 should be allowed under "fair use," with clear attribution. Those from earlier writers are in the public domain. Direct quotes are so indicated by conventional single and double quote marks; and paraphrased or indirect quotes by parentheses or brackets. Omissions from the original texts are indicated by ellipses. Titles are created by the finder. Narrative summaries also, where needed, are supplied by the finder, as are verse line breaks, stanzas, and spacing for rhythms and emphasis of voice. The ambition is to create a new form, while remaining "faithful" to the prose original.

SOURCES

- Sherwood Anderson, *WINESBURG, OHIO*
    (from *"Adventure"*)
- Eudora Welty, *A CURTAIN OF GREEN*
    (from *"Clytie"*)
- Alice Munro, *THE MOONS OF JUPITER*
    (from *"The Moons of Jupiter"*)
- Evan S. Connell, *MRS. BRIDGE*
    (from *"Chapter 45: The Clock"*)
- James Alan McPherson, *ELBOW ROOM*
    (from *"A Loaf of Bread"*)
- Tim O'Brien, *THE THINGS THEY CARRIED*
    (from *"The Things They Carried"*)
- Frank Conroy, *STOP-TIME*
    (from *"Chapter 10: The Coldness of Public Places"*)

- George Orwell, *HOMAGE TO CATALONIA*
  (from *"Chapter XII"*)
- Gustav Flaubert, *MADAM BOVARY*
  (from Part 1, II)
- Tillie Olsen, *TELL ME A RIDDLE*
  (from *"Tell Me A Riddle,"* section 4)
- Ernest Hemingway, *IN OUR TIME*
  (*"Big Two-Hearted River, Part 1"*)
- DeWitt Henry, *THE MARRIAGE OF ANNA MAYE POTTS*
  (from *"The Family House"* and *"Courtship"*)
- DeWitt Henry, *SAFE SUICIDE*
  (from *"Bungee"*)
- Leo Tolstoy, *ANNA KARENINA*
  (from Part VII, Ch XVI)
- Lorrie Moore, *WHO WILL RUN THE FROG HOSPITAL?*
  (sundry)
- George Eliot, *MIDDLEMARCH*
  (from Part 2, Ch. 20)
- Mark Twain, *HUCKLEBERRY FINN*
  (from Ch. 17)
- James Joyce, *"The Dead"*
  (from *DUBLINERS*)
- Raymond Carver, *CATHEDRAL*
  (from *"Where I'm Calling From"*)
- D.H. Lawrence, *WOMEN IN LOVE*
  (from *"Moony"*)
- E.M. Forster, *A PASSAGE FROM INDIA*
  (from Part II—Caves, Chapter XIV)
- Isadora Duncan, *MY LIFE*
  (sundry)
- Jonathan Edwards
  (from *"Sinners in the Hands of an Angry God"*)
- Samuel Richardson, *CLARISSA*
  (from *"Friday, March 3"*)

- Virginia Woolf, *TO THE LIGHTHOUSE*
    (from *"Time Passes"* and *"The Lighthouse"*)
- Samuel Johnson, *"Letter to Lord Chesterfield
    (7th February 1755)"*
- Elizabeth Bowen, *THE DEATH OF THE HEART*
    (from Part II, *"The Flesh,"* Ch 2 & Part III: *"The Devil,"* Ch 3)
- Jonathan Swift, *GULLIVER'S TRAVELS*
    (from *"A Voyage to the Country of the Houyhnhnms,"* Ch. V)
- Robert Coover, *A NIGHT AT THE MOVIES*
    (from *"ROMANCE! You Must Remember This"*)
- Jamaica Kinkaid, *MY BROTHER*
    (from Part 2)

DeWitt Henry

Born in Wayne, PA. Radnor High School, 1959; A.B. Amherst College, 1963; M.A. in English, Harvard University, 1965; Ph.D. English, Harvard University, 1971; completed requirements for M.F.A. University of Iowa, 1968 (did not take the degree).

Founding editor of *Ploughshares* literary magazine, and active editor and director 1971-1995. Interim Director of *Ploughshares* 6/2007-10/2008. Professor Emeritus, Emerson College, 2016-present. Professor, Writing, Literature, and Publishing, Emerson College, 2006-2015; Associate Professor 1989 to 2006: hired as Assistant Professor 1983; Acting Chairperson 1987-8; Chairperson 1989-93.

DeWitt is also a contributing editor to *Solstice: A Magazine of Diverse Voices* (2013-) and to *The Woven Tale Press: Arts and Literary Journal* (2016-).

Also by DeWitt Henry

Fiction

THE MARRIAGE OF ANNA MAYE POTTS
New Edition with Foreword by Margot Livesey
Pierian Springs Press, November 2023
1st Edition, University of Tennessee Press, 2001
(Winner of the **Peter Taylor Prize for the Novel**)

FALLING: SIX STORIES
CreateSpace, 2016

Essays

SWEET MARJORAM: NOTES AND ESSAYS
Plume Editions / MadHat Press, 2018

Memoir

ENDINGS & BEGINNINGS: FAMILY ESSAYS
MadHat Press, 2021
(Long-listed for the **PEN/Diamonstein-Spielvogel Award
for the Art of the Essay**, 2022)

VISIONS OF A WAYNE CHILDHOOD
CreateSpace, 2012

SWEET DREAMS: A FAMILY HISTORY
Hidden River Press, 2011

SAFE SUICIDE: ESSAYS, NARRATIVES, AND MEDITATIONS
Red Hen Press, 2008

Poetry

TRIM RECKONINGS: POEMS
Pierian Springs Press, November 2023

FOUNDLINGS: FOUND POEMS FROM PROSE
New Edition with Notes, Sources & Full Color Art
Pierian Springs Press, October 2023

RESTLESS FOR WORDS: POEMS
Finishing Line Press, February 2023

FOUNDLINGS: FOUND POEMS FROM PROSE
Life Before Man/Gazebo Books, May 2022

Anthologies

SORROW'S COMPANY: WRITERS ON LOSS AND
Beacon Press, 2001

BREAKING INTO PRINT: EARLY STORIES AND
INTO GETTING PUBLISHED; A PLOUGHSHARES A
Beacon Press, 2000

FATHERING DAUGHTERS: REFLECTIONS B
(with James Alan McPherson)
Beacon Press 1998, pb. 1999

OTHER SIDES OF SILENCE: NEW FICTION FROM
Faber and Faber, 1993, o.p.

THE PLOUGHSHARES READER: NEW FICTION
(Winner **Third Annual Editors Book A**
Pushcart Press, 1984, NAL, 1985

Milton Keynes UK
Ingram Content Group UK Ltd.
UKHW020100071123
432073UK00006B/137/J